T0244839

BiOLOGiCiTY

생물성

Biologicity

by Shin Hae-uk

Translated by Spencer Lee-Lenfield

Black Ocean
Boston · Chicago

Copyright © 2024 by Shin Hae-uk
Copyright © 2024 by Spencer Lee-Lenfield
All rights reserved.

생물성
Shin Haewook © 2009
Originally published in 2009 by Moonji Publising Co., Ltd.
All rights reserved.
English translation copyright ©2024

To reprint, reproduce, or transmit electronically, or by recording all or part of this manuscript, beyond brief reviews or educational purposes, please send a written request to the publisher at:

Black Ocean
P.O. Box 52030
Boston, MA 02205
blackocean.org

Cover Art and Design by Abby Haddican | abbyhaddican.com
Book Design by Taylor D. Waring | taylordwaring.com

ISBN: 978-1-939568-93-9
Library of Congress Control Number: 2024934941

This book is published with the support of the Literature Translation Institute of Korea (LTI Korea).

FIRST EDITION

Printed in Canada

CONTENTS

PART 1

PART 2

TRANSLATOR'S FOREWORD

We become most aware of the loneliness of our human bodies when we allow ourselves to daydream beyond their limits. Imagining what it is like to be a bat (as one famous work of philosophy muses), or to have ten eyes rather than two, or a detachable nose, or to be my best friend rather than myself—just the thought makes clear the poverty of our flesh-and-blood experience. What would it be like to be a planet, instead? What might perception feel like, unbound from the neurology of the body as we know it? Rather than endure the torture of thinking about all the possibilities our frail little bodies foreclose from second to second, most of us choose to ignore the topic altogether.

The poetry of Shin Hae-uk reads like a set of letters from someone uniquely horrified by her fellow humans' numbness to the prison of reality and violently committed to waking them to their isolation from the full range of people and objects around them. Loneliness smolders under these words, but only because their speaker hasn't yet given up the possibility of finding others who know the same loneliness. Have you ever imagined what it is like to have the ears of the house you were born in? Do you feel like your mind is a victim of your body's biochemistry? Do you hate your body, but also fear for its safety? Then this book of poems wants you to know you are not alone—or, perhaps, this book wants to be alone, together, with you.

The Korean title of this book, *Saengmulseong*, combines the word *saengmul* (which means "organism," a "living" (*saeng*) "thing" (*mul*), but also serves as the equivalent of the "bio-" half of the Korean word for "biology" (*saengmulhak*)) with the suffix *-seong*, which marks an abstract property (like English "-ness" or "-ity"). We've rendered this as *Biologicity*, a title that should sound as newly coined in English as it does in Korean. The title itself enacts in miniature the poetics orienting the collection: trying to spark, through striking and often odd combinations of familiar parts, recognition of the full strangeness of life as an organic creature bound to a fickle, limited body. "I understand many things / as if they'll burst out from inside me," Shin writes in "On the Dot." We do not fully know ourselves because we haven't reckoned with the weirdness of what lies within us—and so we can't fully know each other, or the world around us. Grappling with our biologicity is no easy task.

These poems are not easy, either. They are hard, at times self-consciously so. They are full of jagged corners and sudden left turns, of a kind now less common in contemporary English poetry than was once the case. Their language swerves from slangy to plaintive, sarcastic to elegant, electric to blue—sometimes across a single break between stanzas. Speakers and tenses are deliberately disorienting at points (for instance, in "Geumja's Salon," "Apart, but Together," and "Debt"), an effect that's part of the way Shin's poetry pushes at the limits of the self. But these poems are also full of rewards. If you find yourself wondering why the speaker of "Birthday, Haply," whose face is de-scrambling itself from a Picasso-like configuration, suddenly goes "mad at the smell of fresh-cooked rice"—I plead patience. If, toward the end of "Angel," the appearance of a flying mouse surprises or confuses you—I plead patience. These are not poems to be downed quickly like pills. They are instead structures to sit with and through which to re-see the world anew. Your question should always be, "How do these strange parts all fit together into a vibrating, oscillating poem?" I promise you: answers will come to those who listen closely.

The promise and the glory of translating such a work as *Biologicity* is that of sharing with readers in English a set of poems with a variety of coherence and a lyric mission entirely different from the kind they already know at home. The work of the literary translator, and especially the translator of poetry, is not the mere movement of words or even sentences from one language into another. No, we are instead translating between two entirely different conceptions of *what a poem is*, what a poem aspires to provide, what constitutes "literary language," and the sum total of the different literary histories informing those ideas and assumptions. The literary English used in poetry has proven relatively stable over roughly the past century; even the difficulty of modernism remains the template for difficulty in our own time. In contrast, Korean has evolved like quicksilver. The vernacular poetry of the 1920s feels linguistically distant from the present in a way more akin to the English of two or three centuries ago. Even the poetic language of the 1980s feels different and distant in texture: vocabulary, script, grammar, and dialect have all shifted dramatically since then. Modern Korean literary history has always been more in touch with the poets of Europe—French, German, Spanish, Russian—than English ever was. And, the contemporary English poets who have entered Korean via translation are a very different group from the greats an American reader might single out.

Moving in the other direction, the picture even an engaged English reader can get of Korean poetry is partial and fragmentary. For all the strides of recent years (especially the phenomenal success that the poetry of Kim Hyesoon has found through her translator Don Mee

Choi), such cardinal modern poets as Ki Hyungdo, Ko Chung-hee, or Oh Kyu-won remain difficult or impossible to read in good translations (or, due to rights situations, to read at all). The poets who make it into print in English translation are, inevitably, refractions of Korean poetry through the taste of English publishers and their readers. That's not a bad thing—it's just the nature of the enterprise. Recognizing this fact means every translation that does make it across is a little message between languages—a nudge to the flux and flow of English from the currents of Korean literature, saying, "This is what a poem is, or can be. This is the language we see as poetic. This is what we ask a great poem to do."

I hope that readers of *Biologicity* will find in it all the power, wit, depth, and charm that Shin Hae-uk's readers in Korean know her for. In her hands, philosophical insights pop out of off-kilter, almost stand-up comedy-like observations, all cast in language that cuts out chaff without idolizing economy. At the same time, I hope readers come— and stay—for a vision of poetry itself different from the poetics now dominant in contemporary English, and also distinct from the Korean poets currently best known in translation. Shin's fellow poet Kim Soyeon has referred to the way her poems suddenly warp and twist as entering "the Shin Hae-uk wormhole." It is a great pleasure to welcome English readers into this vortex.

* * *

A few notes on particular decisions behind this translation, of the sort entailed in every translation between Korean and English:

1. Proper names of people and places have been transliterated using Revised Romanization.

2. Readers may also notice that some titles of individual poems are italicized. Shin sometimes uses a Korean transliteration of an English word to title her poems—for instance, 밀크, "*milkeu*," rather than the Korean word for "milk," *uyu*. I've italicized titles to indicate this effect.

3. Korean offers more flexibility and decisiveness than English does in using its grammar to indicate a change in voices, especially the existence of a "written form" for verbs and its system of formal address. Where multiple speakers are implied, I've sometimes added italics or quotation marks that were not present in the Korean version of the poem.

4. As noted, the use of tense is at times deliberately disorienting. (Korean is also, by convention, somewhat freer in tense than English.) On a few occasions, I have reduced apparent shifts in tense within a single poem for the sake of clarity—though I have never taken them out altogether, especially where there is a clear point to the manipulation of tense. ("Gym Class" is one notable example.)

5. I've generally tried to retain the visual arrangement of Shin's poems, but have occasionally added or dropped a line to a stanza for the sake of prosody, visual or sonic. The second-to-second, minute-to-minute pace of Korean is quicker and lighter than that of English, in a way that makes syllable-to-syllable correspondences deceiving. Traditional Korean prosody tends to use variable "feet" of 3 to 6 syllables as its principal unit of organization—a pulse that one can still feel behind many a contemporary poet working in free verse. In a very loose way, I've tried

to align the number of feet in Korean with the number of accentual pulses in English, though there are many exceptions throughout this work.

6. Korean, like the languages of its neighbors, is rich with sensory-onomatopoeic words with no direct and concise equivalent in English (or many other languages): for instance, *challangchallang*, the sound/look of a cup brimming to the full; *ajjilajjil*, the sound/look of a sudden rush of vertigo; etc. I've adopted several strategies to relay such words, the most striking of which to readers will likely be transliteration or straightforward replication of the sound of the words (as in "*Stop Motion*"). At other times, I've used English words with an onomatopoeic edge ("jangle," "clamber") to bake the emphatic coloration of such words into the main action. Occasionally, English does offer a nearly one-to-one counterpart for Korean, and I've sometimes (but not always) availed myself of those, too.

—SPENCER LEE-LENFIELD

AUTHOR'S NOTE:

I feel as though I've borrowed a tiny bit
of a day with no date or name for my birthday,
and am writing a diary entry about it.
I've had far too little oxygen,
but with great effort, I suppose I managed to breathe,
somehow.

My heartfelt gratitude
to all who read these words.

—Shin Hae-uk
Winter, 2009

Part I

BIRTHDAY, HAPLY

Ears, eyes, mouth, nose exist most of the time as they like—
and today, mine are going back where they belong.

Yet I've never learned how to keep them straight.
I'm becoming me,
and want me
to like me—
but where's this awkward time coming from?

I slowly go mad at the smell of fresh-cooked rice.

I think my life is going to outlast me.

SOME THOUGHTS ON NOT ENDING

Each day I die in someone else's dreams

I'm terrified of ice
melting in hot water

stories quivering
fine as fish roe

I cannot lay out each by each
all the things I love

keep shifting my expressions
thinking about the time where I belong
and all the time that got
away from me

dreaming someone else's dream
laughing someone else's laugh

I'm a patch of odd air, or sometimes
mere memory of a real thing

I shed blood and

I am sadness become human

GEUMJA'S SALON

I put my hair in Geumja's hands.

I see her scissors flit around;
she watches my hair
spill onto the tiles.

My spine is straight and stiff;
the tiles, white.

My hairs, each at its own angle,
are never going to forget today:

I'll become part
of Geumja's time.

She sets both hands on my shoulders,
touches
my neck,
my hair.

But our future selves
might not have been like this.

CATCHER IN THE RYE

Reading a book for class,
I'm soaked in emotion:

that children in pain might not suffer,
and trees dying alone might not feel lonely,

I underline the words with all my heart—
but weep with just one eye.

White letters fill the chalkboard,
moving bit by bit;

sitting in the exact same posture,
I keep reading the exact same line,

protecting those
who just pass by
then leave.

I flash my teeth and feel like grinning.
Just like *Jaws*.

APART, BUT TOGETHER

Let's share a name from now on.
Perfectly equal:

till now, our time together
has been too selfish, too lonely.

We both have two eyes,
a pair of ears,
countless hairs—but

my share of things
doesn't work like that:

the lines on my palm run where they like,
then vanish just the same;

the people in my dreams
stretch into reality, answer the phone;

and I'm bad at subtraction—
I don't get how some things just remain,
while others disappear.

If we share a name,
I won't be stalked,
I'll hear no double sounds:

Let's think it over.

RAILROAD

1. THERE IS A TRAIN:

it's long,

and as it stretches onward,
the sunshine starts to falter.

Further
and further backward I step;
I swear I can feel the very earth.

I'm far away.

2. I AM A PERSON.

The hours dissolve
along with my smile.

But why can't I revert
back to being me,
a human back to a human?

3. I UNDERSTAND THE TRAIN.

It keeps on stretching.

Its shadow, bit by bit, grows
longer, fainter.

Between this summer and the next
there runs another summer. Lightly,
horribly.

THE HOUSE OF HANSEL AND GRETEL'S WITCH SPEAKS

Aren't my ears pointy?

Candy killed me, but now
I'm turning into even stinkier candy;

air leeches to my arms, then won't slough off—
lizardlike weather. I'm frozen in place

longing for a kiss:

purple lipstick doubles my lips in size,
but I catch each trace of salt,
as if in endless water.
They say you can have twice the smile...

So if someone said they'd like to be *my* house,
I'd bid them a cool
Good morning.

Before my limbs, like butter, melt away.
Before my head, like water, turns clear.

WHITE

It's cold.
I don't want to be catalogued:

I only have one heart,

but my face is white as the snow
and as multiple as its flakes.

I can't take off my black wig,

and even when I put on see-through slippers,
I never disappear.

I'm always a smidge different from yesterday.

I listen
to my own
watery breathing:

I'm deep in unwanted thoughts
and today just keeps on ending.

It's cold.

COLOR

I suffer from excessive colors.
I've been bad;
there were so many things I liked
that I kept stealing them:
natural,
artificial—
sorry, I even messed with your shadow,
and worse, stole from the water.

The colors fill me oddly,
so my knees bend too easily;
my eyeballs are enormous,
and I
am far too heavy.
But still, there's many an upside:
you are here,
I am rusting,
and short of breath.

It'll be like this
a long, long time.

THE TALE OF MARIE

Marie has a face.
I have a face, too, but I also
have a lot of work to do.

Her face is pink.
When I jump fast, my teeth clatter,
but her mouth has no teeth.

She has to strain to smile.
In the dark—no smile.
Though I'm there—no smile.

When she's sad, beyond mere tears,
it's like she's pouring out her dark black eyes.

I have to think about what's next,
but I wish it were me and not Marie
trying to learn to smile with my face.

Soon she too will have to grow up.
Still. Time is always short,
and birthdays blow by like the breeze.

ANGEL

My back is itchy.

In one hand, I hold a white stone;
in the other, an umbrella.

It's raining outside the umbrella.

Slowly, I crane
my head over one shoulder
to look behind my back:

it's raining there, too.

My shadow's wet;
for a moment,
I'm almost sad.

It wants to speak,
like a creature of flesh and blood
with sense perceptions.

A white mouse pops
from my hand;

if it flies
I think I'll take off, too.

TO A FRIEND I MISS

I'm drafting a letter in the hand of a friend who died at twelve:

Hello. Friend. I'm still
eating food in my human form,
thinking with my human brain.

Yet today—today, I realized:
I'd like to lend myself to you,

want to break out your smile
after three years in deep-freeze.

If you want,
you can put my
voice on tape.

My hand might move awkwardly,
but I do believe if I were you
I'd be up to writing your story.

I hope you'll write me back.

Hello. Friend.
I like you—
like a tottering bowling pin.

SECRETS AND LIES

No one knows I'm a gymnast now.

Arms, legs stuffed into my clothes,
I walk along like no big deal.

I can only stretch my limbs out when I sleep,
an outrage, but
can skip rope ropelessly at night.
Not too shabby.

As I jump, I don't go slack,
but my hang time does,
just a bit.
No sudden
snapping back to myself.

This world always needs
just one more gymnast:
my heart leaps up,

an all-too-beautiful, transparent feat
that no one sees at all.

NOT MY CONVERSATION

I've got two eyes—
with one, I look left,
with the other, right.

To my left, a window;
my right, a fishbowl.

Even at night, fish
can only live in water.

As if I'd had a fish eye transplant,
even in my sleep, I watch
the world with eyes wide open.

Even in there
the trees have leaves,
I have a backside.

The speed I'm talking at today
is different from yesterday,

no links between the conversations.

I have two eyes. But they do get lonely.

GOODMORNING

Today the sun came out.
And so, today
I get to be a brighter person.

I press my baseball cap down hard
and do a 180°
with my face.

I bury my eyes deep in my hat,
lips grinning like a doll
whose smile survives a gunshot,

and if I eat a real breakfast,
I'll be able to keep talking
like I have a second throat.

Maybe I'll play piano
as if I have a wizard's hands.

I'll slide on white gloves,
stretch out all ten fingers.

I'm turning into a lover of the truth.

MY LENGTH

I lengthen easily,
unpredictably,
like a story.

But my work is always out of reach.

No matter how hard I throw,
the classroom stays a square;
but its shadows silently stretch toward the window;
and, in my yellow armband,

I just walk wherever my backbone leads,
no matter how deep it hunches.

Should you see Yu Gwansun[1] in the hall,
just pass with a nod of the head.

Today's an anniversary that will only happen once.

My thoughts flow where I go,
and no matter who you are,
I'm the same age as you.

STOP MOTION

If you want to think,
think of home.

The walls blur together then
SSSTOP,

and *mu'ROCK! mu'ROCK!*—
a home pops up inside them,

and in those thoughts,
there I am.

Yet in my thoughts,
there's something drawing ever closer.
Bit by bit—

"We need one more person in this house."

But my home—

I look back, and
once more SSSTOP.

If home came crumbling down inside my thoughts:

did I become myself, then get born?
Or was I born before I was really me?

CLOSE-UP

My mouth's so big it could swallow my face.
It'd be nice to hand my teeth to the dentist
and go hang out somewhere else.

But my lips keep clinging to my head.
They say, don't get hung up on size—
or sometimes, don't worry you're wet
if you're already in the sea.

Though my teeth don't wiggle when I brush,
when I go to sleep, I feel as though
they're rotting out from eating too much chocolate.

This ragged look will leak off my face.
Even duct tape
won't keep it on.

Even apart from my face,
I'm growing uncontrollably.

A TALE OF EYES

1. BEING ONE PERSON AT A TIME IS GOOD ENOUGH

Each day, I open different eyes.

Morning never fails to break;

and the days my eyes open when I want
brim full of grace.

But even when I have to prise open eyes
that crave to stay shut, I want
a kiss.

2. NOT BEING ABLE TO BE ONE PERSON AT A TIME IS KIND OF SAD

I shall put on my t-shirt with the eyeball silkscreen print,
and from tomorrow, turn into a giant dragonfly.

Today is my
very last day.

My eyes' last glance
turns out the window—

my eyes upon eyes, and
ever more eyes in my eyes.

Like a dragonfly with its wings torn off,
morning comes in for a crash landing.

3. I'VE GOT A FAVOR

It does not do merely to open one eye in advance
and act like a little bit of a person.

Mom's sad enough to cry,
but as for me,
I – *cannot* – wipe away – clear liquids.

We cannot even cry together.

FAMILY OF WATER

Today for lunch
I ate fish food

because it was hard to think of fish
with their elegant, gracile necks.

I sketch the curve of my own on paper,
and wait a long time
till my hunger passes.

Paper sinks in water,
but dead fish float.

It would be nice if I
could sing some humdrum song,
then eat salt with those fishes.

ON THE DOT

I found my center of gravity.
Inhaling, I feel
my flesh sticking to my bones;
thinking, I feel
my blood silently churning.

Night falls.

I understand many things
as if they'll burst out from inside me.

*

So, like Pluto, I trace an ellipse,
unsure how long I can keep running.
Even if they say that Pluto has vanished,
Pluto can't just shift its course alone.
Even if Pluto loses its name,
Pluto doesn't care.

*

Doesn't care at all.

*

My fingernails are growing.

Anyway—I wasn't sure
if even my time didn't want to come back.

TIMES TABLE

I memorized the times table.

Aus Eins mach Zehn
Und Zwei laß gehn
Und Drei mach gleich...
Verlier die Vier!
Aus Fünf und Sechs...
Mach Sieben und Acht...[2]

Cat's lives are nine.
Fingers are five + five =
ten.

The times table teems with life,
and I'm becoming a number.

Just as nine fingers
would be one too few,
even out of nine,
cats don't have an extra life
to lend to humans.

Und Neun ist Eins,
Und Zehn ist keins.

You've got to cut off your last finger
and toss it to the cat.

I can only do the tables from memory up to nine.

I've got too much blood on my hands to count.

ONE HUNDRED PERCENT HOUSE

A house where no one lives
needs someone to draw it full of glass,
then smash that glass to bits.

Glass is clear
no matter what kind,
so filling it with fingerprints is fine,
scribbling names over names,
pressing to it lip upon lip.

Then just like that
the glass, impassive, will vanish.
The house again
will fill with houseness.

In its air
our traces linger, teeming;
several layers of sighs resound,
and some single shattered shard
might well glint nearby.

And then if the tree to the side
oozes out a human soul—
carve it eyes, nose, lips bright into the bark.

Should you ask, *Who is it?*
I'll tell you, *It's me.*

RINGTONE

I got a strange call.

"Hold on. Coming right now."

*

Hold on. Coming right now.

*

I fell silent, as if colonized.

I put the phone in my other hand
and figured I (and both my hands)
must have been like that from the start.

Part 2

Part 2

EARS

Ears: having just a few more would be great.

Water melting into water—
within that sound,
forever in thought I wanted to sink.

LUNCHTIME

I ate some curry

and had this thought:
Why do I like quiet food?
Do deer find curry tasty?

*

I looked out the window.

On the road, the white outline of a human body
run over by cars a long time,
hit by the rain a long time, too.

No one around to see me,
I stopped,
lost my timing,
held my breath.

*

I drank yesterday's water.

How to get wet in the rain?
I couldn't remember.

FACE OFF[3]

1. CONSOLATION

I had a guest from overseas.

He pulled a face like Hamlet's uncle,
slowly stirring
frozen lips:

"Even the dead need laughter."

I played it off like Hamlet:

"... okay, then."

A terse grin crept over
my lips, then vanished.

2. SOMETHING IN MY FACE SHIFTED

That irritated grin wriggled like a bug;

hidden as if dead,
somewhere
sporadically it squirmed.

I'm being punished, that I might understand.

3. SMILE OFF FACE

Awful.
I shook my head hard.

Like jacks my molars
rattled and cracked in my skull.

Say *cheese* and smile.

4. TIME OFF FACE

Winter's here, and I
have no lips left.

If my teeth freeze, they'll be hard;
my face growing steadily heavier—

but that hasn't happened yet.

We might get snow.
I might have guests.

THE DAY THE PAINT DIDN'T DRY

I forged a pact that day with my watery gaze.

I dipped my middle finger in the water,
drew a circle,
washed a brush and dried it in the sun.

But my pact still isn't dry.

                *

If not wet with water, my soul would be steeped in loneliness.

My blood was heavy,
my eyes were weak;

I needed unerased paper,
transparent faith.

That's how that day went for me.

SIBLINGS

I left behind my little sister there and woke alone.

Like an herbivore's dream
the berries on the tree gaped open,
and my bated breath hung
among gelid specks of oxygen.

It was cold.

*

We have to move house;
but she has to drink milk for sturdy bones

and bury her dead doll.

*

If my eyes were green, how much grass would there have been?
If her teeth were sharp, how would the blood have smelled?

*

I'm buying a cactus
so I can pack
without her;

to stop the plants around her
from drawing any closer,

I clutch her dolly's hands instead.

END OF THE EARTH

Memory, dry as a berry—

I heard one
dripping
out of me,

head lightening
as if full of hydrogen.

*

It clutched at my throat;

I couldn't bear to leave this earth.

Velocity of water falling on Jupiter,
nameless planetesimals—that kind of
blue-skies research
isn't me at all.

My imagination's far too feeble;
slice off my fingers, and the powder will fly

and fail to melt into whatever water it falls.

*

Only my shadow is tall.

The rain falls
on it, even
yesterday.

As it clutches at my throat
we're apart, yet also together.

A SENSE OF THE PAST

Struck on the back,
I turned my head:

If not one thing,
it'll be another. And that's the way it is.

Hands in pockets,
I rattled and clacked my human-ish feelings
a few at a time.

What would I tend to do
if I were human at times like this?

Weird.

There's so much time;
it feels like so long
not to have died yet—

but I'm still
no taller.

HANDS

I put my gloves on.

My hands, absurdly, shrank,
and then, set on my knees,
looked all the stranger.

*

What I envied
wasn't you,
but your tender fingers—

you hold my hand
with them,
touch my face,
then yours.

Why can't love be for three.

Why isn't there anything
in this world but you
and me.

*

I took the gloves off, touched the window.

Peel your hands off gently
and your palmlines stick to the glass,
and might spread where they will.

But destiny awaits you.
Let's tape the glass so it doesn't break,
and keep our gloves on.

*

Two hands inside these gloves.
One is mine.
I wish the other were yours.

TASTE

How was my dream? So sweet
I feel my teeth rotting, face melting.

Take my hand. Please.

Your spoon tastes different from mine,
yet we share the same hopes.

When I hold your round warm hand,
I feel like I'm eating pancakes

as winter comes.

I'm more than willing to wait.

No wings, no premonitions were ready
for us—but god, our hands fit right.

PANTS PROBLEMS

I want to try your jeans on.

They look like they were made for me—
I can't turn away,

my feelings in shambles
as I slowly picture
my legs
in your jeans.

I put my hands in my back pockets,
lock my knees,

lean your head
on my shoulder.

When I'm good and you're not,
it pains me.

When I need a second face on top of mine,
will you lend me yours?

Sorry—

but I think my legs are about to fuse,
like a mermaid's.

GYM CLASS

When gym draws near
my gym clothes vanish,
my sweat streams down.

My clothes are wet;
I'm heavy
as if there were two of me.
But with no gym clothes,
I choose to hide
behind the back
of my skinniest friend.
I do the warm-ups
like nothing at all;

my friend gets dizzyheaded,
stained with my sweat,
her body, too, a mess,
my hands, feet ever more useless.
No nosebleed when you need it...

Gym time
keeps going on, constantly almost over,

and now I actually have to hold my breath.
I hate it when my gym clothes reappear,
leaving me alone.
You can't catch your breath
on your own very well.

WORLD OF FOSSILS

You look just great.
I'm wrapping a bandaid around my finger.

The room is close to a still life,
but my finger, *au contraire*,
thrashes and throbs like it has a life of its own.

This finger brings chaos.

If a snake with shattered spine skittered over the floor,
its print would be damp
but my hands would be tied.

If I pour water on my favorite pebble,
at night it might suddenly swell into a boulder
and then come rolling toward me.
Scary, right?

Yet you aren't scared;
you look just great.

Yet what can come for me
can also come for you.

My finger might understand
the way you're headed.

THE NIGHT BEFORE EASTER

Watch out:
you'll be punished
if you salt your Easter eggs,

the neighbor told me.

His visit was unexpected,
but he'd led a clever life
rich with experiences.

I took his hand,
and sobbed and asked,
What if the salt has lost its saltiness?

His hand was slick;
his eyes (I think)
had cataracts.

If so, tell me,
how should I
face tomorrow?

What if I married him instead?

Boiling eggs now, I imagine

his mouth,
and Lazarus eating a fertilized egg,
and worry about my future.

SCARF

It smelled awful inside my head.
But to plug my nose and air it out was far too hard,
and I couldn't tell orange
from pink, hair
from thread.

I started knitting each day—in my head.
Bamboo needles, warm
string, left then
right hands calmly
winding some days
into three
rows, others
seven: I could
see them.

Stop thinking, and the scarf vanished,
dried raindrops drifted back.
Play dumb, right then left
hands, clear today
and yesterday—just like that,
thought stitched to thought,
my scarf stretched longer,
the smell no worse,

and I was grateful.
As if I suddenly understood hair properly,
my shoulders broadened,
my neck stretched a touch longer.

GUEST

Monday's already on its way.

When Tuesday passes,
my room won't reek of human,
and though I'm no Wednesday,
I'll fill its place
by taking off my clothes.

Since I've hardly any height
I can rob my whole room
through a crack in the door—
edges sides angles—
and then, free from Wednesday and from me,
that room will be
quintessentially
quadrilateral.

Wouldn't it be great if I could hug my room,
rub my face all over every wall?–

That desire seizes me;
I'm still not Wednesday
but it embraces me instead,
and though I can stand the shame
I count, not knowing

how high the number will go,
and wait for something like Monday.

But someone out there loved
this room before I did.
Someone tall.
Before it had a nick or scratch,
free from fear of Wednesdays and gravity.

TEXTURE

He had not a knot in his handwriting,

but I just had to unravel his cursive,
weave long clothes with it.

We pretend we don't
know each other,

but my scent lingers
on those clothes,

which perfectly fit
his stiffening body.

                *

As if my thoughts had bones,
he turns into a whole person,

a story so clear
his bones are visible,
more than mere bones,
at my fingertips.

Only thoughts on knots
remain regrets.

BIOLOGICITY

I wore a white patch on one eye
and a white face mask.

"Even mice and dogs have faces," I thought,
then felt ludicrous, ashamed,
deflated.

I listened to rabbits' voices:
I'm albino. And you?

"Go away, please." I forced
my one eye shut.

       *

My mouth was growing sicker bit by bit.

Two words appeared at once,
but I couldn't guess where they were heading.
I couldn't move my teeth,
couldn't move my jaw to chew.

But my cheekbones worked.

       *

Maybe I'm rehearsing
to capture wild animals that escaped their cages.

I'd been training,
but the faces required were beyond imagination.

I tucked an extra mask
and patch into my pocket,

too weak to stand
faceless misfortune.

TIME OF WET HAIR

He washed my hair with his hands;

soft as a chicken sexer's,
they cradled the problems burning
in my brain.

I wanted to strap on a helmet and escape

but my brain
got in my way,
so with his hands
still wet, he plugged up both my ears.

My head was so phlegmatic
I didn't know how to hold myself,
felt such shame I couldn't stand still.

IN LINE

This was orderly progress:

one person, one line each,
and nothing,
no one else,
beyond the forward march.

But I had a front and a back.

I shook my head hard,
thinking this would not do.

Am I not also a human?

But without a hand to help,
soon I lost my way.

"What do you expect of a mixed-blood kid?"

I felt dizzy, as if stabbed,

two kinds of blood flowing from me,

clear as lies.

For checking others' blood
was growing necessary.

SOUND

In my ears today,
the sound of paper ripping—

one sheet,
colorless,
evidently edgeless—

yet precious all the same,
or so it seemed.

I felt it would be wrong
not to fold it up and keep it.

I lean toward wondering

should I rip off an ear
and throw it at the sound.

It'll only bleed a bit,
and I'll put my trust in the other,

like a day
with half an hour deleted.

HALF+

It wasn't like this at first.

It wrapped its arm around my left,
hounding me
to write left-handed.

Put down my arm!

And then, in white colored pencil on a blank sheet
it took what I dictated:

Master calligrapher.

I wanted to tear it up
but the decision was out of my hands.

My left was obviously lacking.
It knew me all too well.

"It wasn't like this at first."

Its left hand bit by bit
burrowed deep into my right.

It felt like folding my own hands,
barely a feeling at all,
and I got lost in thoughts
of how I'd been at first.

WATER AND BLOOD

I was bleeding,

throat drying
from all the things on my mind.

The time had come
to take better care of it.

*

One of my fingers twitched,
then started to erase
my ears,
eyes, mouth,
nose, one
by one—

then sketched the thoughts
running through my blood
onto my newly blank face.

I've got to drink some water—
drink water and then
with all my strength
finally get away from this finger—

I've got to open my eyes.

                *

But first
I bled.
You can't drink water ahead of time.

What if I
grow out my teeth to guard my neck,
sharp as the winter chill?

Yet even this idea
is already mixed
with blood.

MILK

My hand stank like fish,

so I need to stop using it for a while,

have to consider the beauty of what I eat,

prepare to drink palely curdled milk.

What else can I do?

Had my hand been wet
I'd have chopped it off
to chill it in the fridge—

if hot, I'd use its blood as ink,
and smell that instead.

THE BUTCHER'S SHOP

Like he's about to gallop off
he flashes an enormous grin,
hawking meat.

Nothing for me to deny.

But I'm barehanded,
with arms too short
to deal with his grin:

no matter how far I stretch,
I can't get them to pop
off my shoulders,
and his smile
drips from my fingers with his blood.

He believes me no matter what,
so what am I to do?

Why are there
no words for his disappointment?

SACK

He breathes like he has no lungs.

I hug my sack full of objects close
and keep on working without a blink.

*

"This is no place for you to be,"

he says as he shoves me into a room
full of breathing furniture,

plunging me into shit-filled dreams.

He likes to watch me flailing in
a pillow stuffed with teeming hair.

Some countries are too big.
A map can't comprehend them.

*

I manage to snatch the sack away.

I can't breathe
inside it.
I've got more work to do.

DEBT

I borrowed the body
of an angel.

Though it's not like mine hadn't been good enough,
a fraction of time
made clear my own was an awful situation.

An angel's body—
I was more than a little obsessed with my debt,

could barely breathe with the wings,
had no clue what to do
with their weight upon my shoulders.

The angel half-smiled at my backside
and said, *You must bury yourself
in thoughts whiter than snow.*

*Angel bodies are worth more
than mere money,
and since they last longer than time itself,
there's no real way to repay them.*

Only a few times in life
have I ever

seen an expression as useless as mine.

Even in my face, hardened
to the point of breaking,

an angel's tears
blot out the way ahead.

GUEST BOOK

To the address next door
came a white wig
and a second face:

an invitation to a world full of humans
just the same as me.

And so
I have to wash my face.

                *

Once clean,
I look for the house next door,

then, foot still on the sill,
I don the wig
over my second face
with a pained expression:

"Actually, this isn't me."

                *

Behind it,
my face was staring holes into my back.

Let's go back to our place.
At home, we've got
so many names.

NOTES

1. Yu Gwansun was executed at age sixteen in 1919 for her role in organizing the movement for independence from the Japanese Empire. Because she has been remembered as a national hero in Korea, for many years her portrait was hung in classrooms, especially in girls' schools.

2. The German in this poem comes from the "Witches' Multiplication Table" in Goethe's Faust. In the Korean version of the poem, it appears in Korean translation, with a citation. I reproduce it here in German advisedly.

3. There is a pun at work throughout this poem. In Korean, the title is 얼굴 外, meaning "outside," "off," "besides," or "except the face." But it sounds like the common(er) phrase 얼굴 왜, meaning "Why is your face [like that]?"—something you'd ask a person who looks distraught or otherwise troubled or out of the normal. I've tried to keep a sense of wordplay through the multiple meanings of "Face Off," including the subtitles of sections 3 and 4. But it's not quite the same as the wordplay in the Korean.

TRANSLATOR'S ACKNOWLEDGMENTS

Many thanks to the poet, Shin Hae-uk, for these wonderful poems, and for entrusting me with her work in English. Shin also read every draft of this translation along with me, and addressed each of my questions, no matter how microscopic in nature. I owe my introduction to Shin's work to the poet Yu Heekyung, proprietor of the Seoul bookshop Wit & Cynical, whose readings, workshops, and other events provide a crucial nexus for poets in the city and beyond.

Many hands helped make this translation the best it could be. My friend Joey Junsu Hong played the crucial role of an external translation editor, reading the English word-by-word alongside the Korean to fix my errors of understanding. Fellow translators Soje, Paige Aniyah Morris, and Moon Hoyoung read early drafts of these translations in summer 2021 and provided help and encouragement. Madeleine Schwartz, Jonathan Chan, and Evan Eschliman read the English in its own right, with detailed notes. Talin Tahajian turned a practiced poet's eye on the manuscript in a late phase. The attention of Cindy Juyoung Ok at *Guernica* benefited in particular the poem "One Hundred Percent House," which first ran in that magazine. My spouse, the writer Yung In Chae, helped me parse a number of intransigent lines in a late draft. Jake Levine of Black Ocean helped save me from a number of near-errors. All remaining mistakes are my own.

I thank all those who have taught me translation in theory and practice through the years, especially Peter Cole, Emily Greenwood, Robyn Creswell, Samuel Perry, and Jeffrey Angles.

I am grateful to the journals that have previously published some of these poems, occasionally in versions slightly different from those printed here: *Acta Koreana*, the Asian American Writers' Workshop *The Margins*, *The Dial*, *Guernica*, *Kenyon Review*, and *New England Review*.

ABOUT THE AUTHOR:

Shin Hae-uk is the author of three poetry books in Korean in addition to essay collections and a novel. She won Korea's Author's Choice Emerging Poet Award in 2010 and received the Kim Hyun Literary Prize in 2022. She holds a doctorate in Korean literature from Korea University and currently teaches creative writing at Dongduk Women's University in Seoul.

ABOUT THE TRANSLATOR:

Spencer Lee-Lenfield's translations from Korean to English have appeared in publications including *Guernica*, *New England Review*, *Colorado Review*, *Asymptote*, and *The Dial*. Lee-Lenfield is currently a Ph.D. candidate in comparative literature at Yale University as well as an assistant editor at *The Yale Review*. Lee-Lenfield's writing has appeared in *PMLA*, *Modern Language Quarterly*, *Poetics Today*, *The New York Review of Books*, *The Chronicle of Higher Education*, *Harvard Magazine*, and *Slate*.

ABOUT THE SERIES

The Moon Country Korean Poetry Series publishes new English translations of contemporary Korean poetry by both mid-career and up-and-coming poets who debuted after the IMF crisis. By introducing work which comes out of our shared milieu, this series not only aims to widen the field of contemporary Korean poetry available in English translation, but also to challenge orientalist, neo-colonial, and national literature discourses. Our hope is that readers will inhabit these books as bodies of experience rather than view them as objects of knowledge, that they will allow themselves to be altered by them, and emerge from the page with eyes that seem to see "a world that belongs to another star."